Powe

The PowerShell for Beginners Guide to Learn PowerShell Scripting, PowerShell 5 and Windows PowerShell

By

Matthew Adams

Contents

Introduction

I want to thank you and congratulate you for purchasing the book, ***"PowerShell: The Powershell for Beginners Guide To Learn Powershell Scripting, Powershell 5 and Windows Powershell."***

This book contains proven steps and strategies on how to go from being a beginner to an expert at PowerShell.

Anyone can learn PowerShell and how to use it, but it takes some hard work and dedication to become an expert. This book will cover the basics of PowerShell, the components that you need to know to use it and will also provide you with some exercises to test your knowledge and help you to better learn how to use PowerShell to its full potential.

Thanks again for purchasing this book, I hope you enjoy it!

.

Chapter 1

The Basics of PowerShell

Most of us have heard of a command prompt and we know, roughly, what to do with it, but fewer people are aware of PowerShell, a tool that is so much more powerful than a simple command prompt and, in many ways, is expected to take the place of the prompt. This is because PowerShell gives us more control and more power with the Windows Operating system. But what exactly is it?

In terms of computers, a shell is an interface that provides you with access to some different services offered by the operating system and a shell can be a simple command-line or it can have a full graphical user interface (GUI). Windows PowerShell was developed by the Redmond Giants and Microsoft to help with configuration management and to automate certain tasks. It is based on .NET and has both a command line and PowerShell ISE, which stands for Integrated Scripting Environment. This is a GUI that lets users create different scripts easily without the need to type loads of commands in.

PowerShell was designed to speed up and automate several administrative tasks, for example, showing the USB devices that are installed on a network or a computer, or setting up a task that takes a lot of time to run in the background while you do something else. You can also use it as a way of identifying processes that have stopped responding and kill them. All of this is done by creating scripts and putting multiple commands together.

A History of PowerShell

PowerShell was created when Microsoft identified a need for something more than the Command Prompt offered, something that would help users to automate some processes and make life easier and more productive.

PowerShell was first released in 2006 for Windows XP, Vista and Microsoft Server 2003. It was originally designed for increasing productivity in high volume areas, for those who had several tasks that needed doing but simply didn't have the time to do them all. PowerShell is designed to remove the menial tasks and increase productivity in different environments.

Through the years, Microsoft has released 4 versions of PowerShell to coincide with the changes in their operating system, bringing us to PowerShell 5.0.

How to Get PowerShell

If you are on Windows 7 or later, PowerShell is already built into your operating system. It is, however, not visible so you will need to search for it. Simply bring up the search bar and type in PowerShell and it will appear in the menu. You can create a shortcut to it and pin it to your taskbar or start menu so it is easier to find in the future – simply right-click the icon and choose the option you want.

It is worth noting that PowerShell 5 comes as standard with Windows 10; earlier operating systems will be in the earlier versions of PowerShell so you will need to upgrade and anyone on earlier than Windows 7 will need to install PowerShell 5 manually.

Upgrading or Installing PowerShell

PowerShell 5 is a part of WMF – Windows Management Framework – version 5 and WMF needs .NET Framework 4.4 to install it. That means having to install this package before you can upgrade to or install PowerShell 5 on a Windows 7 or Server 2008 PC. If you are already using Windows 8, Server 2012, or higher, you will already have .NET 4.5 on your machine. Just to make sure, bring up the Command Prompt and type in the following – it will show what version is installed:

```
(Get-ItemProperty -Path 'HKLM:\SOFTWARE\Microsoft\NET
Framework Setup\NDP\v4\Full').Version
```

If this command gives you a missing registry key error, it means 4.5 is not installed.

Before You Install

Before you go ahead and install there are some things you should know. There are applications, like SharePoint that are dependent on specific versions of PowerShell. For example, if you created some scripts and then upgraded SharePoint server, your scripts will break.

While most of the code that is built for earlier PowerShell versions will work, in some cases, PowerShell 5 is just different enough that it can cause problems. Most of these are likely to come with external dependencies, such as SharePoint or those vendors that have not updated their PowerShell support code.

How to Install or Upgrade PowerShell 5

Before you can do anything, you must download the installer, making sure you get the right one for your specific system. The following each have their own downloads on https://msdn.microsoft.com/en-us/PowerShell/wmf/5.0/requirements. If you do, try to install the wrong one you will get a warning message. Once the download has completed, you can upgrade your system or install the new version.

Find the installer you just downloaded and double-click it. Follow the instructions on the screen to install the KB for your system – it will be called Update for Windows (KBXXXXXXX).

When that is installed, you will See PowerShell as being installed under that heading in Programs and Features. Confirm that you want to upgrade, click to accept the EULA and leave the installer to do its job.

When it has finished, you will need to reboot your system to finish the installation and, when your system starts up again, just double-check to confirm the installation went OK. To do this, open PowerShell console and type in `$PSVersionTable.PSVersion`. If all went smoothly, under Major property, you will see 5.

Post Installation

Once PowerShell is installed, you need to configure it to run scripts. Normally, scripting will be disabled by default but you will only need to do the following once.

- Open PowerShell by right-clicking the icon and selecting "Run as Administrator"
- PowerShell will open a command prompt so type in the following command: `PS> Set-ExecutionPolicy RemoteSigned` – make sure you don't close the Shell down and you will need it again

To edit your profile, type the following at the prompt:

```
PS> New-Item -Path $Profile -ItemType file -Force

PS> notepad $Profile

PS> exit
```

You do not need to open PowerShell as administrator anymore, you only needed to do that to set up the execution policy. From now on you can run it normally.

Configuring the Console

The PowerShell console gives you an easy environment for running commands and creating script files for running later. You can leave it exactly as it is or you can configure it to your own personal taste. For example, you may want to change the font size, background color or expand the buffer size. There are several ways to do this in PowerShell – either from the command window, using PowerShell commands or by adding scripts to your profile so that the settings are applied automatically whenever you start up.

Configuring Console Properties

The appearance of PowerShell is determined by the default or user-defined settings in a shortcut that is then passed into PowerShell executable as an argument. To modify the property settings:

- Click on the PowerShell icon in the console window – top left corner
- Click on Properties
- Now you will see 4 tabs – Colors, Layout, Font, Options

Click on each one to make the changes you require:

- **Options** – settings for command history and cursor size. Choose from 2 editing options – QuickEdit, which allows you to copy and paste commands using your mouse or Insert, which will not overwrite text in a line, rather inserting it instead.
- **Font** – Here you can change the size and style of the font, although choices are limited
- **Layout** – Choose the size of the buffer, window and the position of the window. Buffer size is for setting the number of characters and the number of lines in the buffer – this can be equal to or larger than the window size but not smaller. Window size is for determining the actual height and width of the window and position lets you choose where to place the console window on the desktop.
- **Colors** – Choose the color you want for your background and text

Once you have made the changes you want, close the Properties box by clicking OK and all changes will be immediately applied. These changes will remain as they are only if you open PowerShell from the same place that you opened it originally. If you want the changes to stay, regardless of where you open PowerShell from, you need to do something different and that is how to script your settings. Here is an example of what you can do:

Open your notepad window (your text editor) and type in this code:

```
Set-Alias rc Edit-PowerShellProfile


function Prompt

{

    $mywd = (Get-Location).Path

    $mywd = $mywd.Replace( $HOME, '~' )

    Write-Host "PS " -NoNewline -ForegroundColor
DarkGreen

    Write-Host ("" + $mywd + ">") -NoNewline -
ForegroundColor Green

    return " "

}


function Edit-PowerShellProfile
```

```
{
    notepad $Profile
}
```

Save it and then open PowerShell – the changes should be evident as you have saved this as a profile script. Now you can customize to your heart's content and, when you want to open your profile in notepad, simply type “rc” at the command prompt. Remember to save any changes you make and launch PowerShell for the changes to take effect.

PowerShell IDE

IDE stands for Integrated Development Environment and is the tool of choice for computer programmers and software developers. The IDE will have a source code editor, a debugger, and several build automation tools. There are several different ones that you can use for PowerShell but by far the best, and easiest to use, is the integrated ISE.

The Integrated Scripting Environment in PowerShell is a host application and you can use it for running commands, writing, testing and debugging in a single GUI. That GUI contains the following features:

- Multiline editing
- Tab completion
- Syntax coloring

- Selective execution
- Context-sensitive help
- Right-to-Left language support

There are shortcut items and menu items that can help you to carry out many of the exact same tasks that you would otherwise do in a PowerShell Console. For example, if you debugged a script that was in the ISE, you could set a line breakpoint in it by right-clicking the code line and clicking on Toggle Breakpoint. Other things you can do are:

- **Multiline Editing** – In the Command pane, you can insert a blank line beneath the current line by pressing SHIFT+ENTER
- **Selective Execution** – If you want to run a part of your script, select the specific text and click on Run Script of press on F5
- **Context-Sensitive Help** – Just type in Invoke-Item and press on F1. The Help file will open to the specific topic relating to the Invoke-Item cmdlet. The same applies to any item that you want help on

You can also customize certain aspects of the ISE appearance and there is a specific PowerShell profile where functions, variables, aliases and commands can be stored.

To open Windows PowerShell ISE:

Either:

- Click on Start>All Programs>Windows PowerShell>Windows PowerShell ISE, OR
- Open the PowerShell console CMD.exe or type PowerShell_ise.exe in the Run box

PowerShell Profiles

A PowerShell profile is a script that will run whenever a new PowerShell session is started. There are 6 profiles supported in Windows PowerShell 5 and they are used to configure the console environment, such as configuring aliases, loading modules, defining functions or simply changing the size of the font on your console.

Both PowerShell ISE and PowerShell console have their own profiles and there are also profiles for each user and for the current user. These are the 6 profiles and their locations:

1. Current User, Current Host – console - `$Home\[My ]Documents\WindowsPowerShell\Profile.ps1`
2. Current User, All Hosts - `$Home\[My ]Documents\Profile.ps1`
3. All Users, Current Host – console - `$PsHome\Microsoft.PowerShell_profile.ps1`
4. All Users, All Hosts - `$PsHome\Profile.ps1`
5. Current user, Current Host – ISE - `$Home\[My ]Documents\WindowsPowerShell\Microsoft.PowerShellISE_profile.ps1`

6. All users, Current Host – ISE - *$PsHome\Microsoft.PowerShellISE_profile.ps1*

The first thing you should understand about these profiles is that they move and, provided you keep that in mind, you will get on just fine with them. Most of the time, when we talk about the PowerShell profile, we are talking in terms of the Current User or Current Host profile.

The $profile Variable

Whenever you query $profile, which is an automatic variable, the path will be returned to Current User, Current Host profile. This does make sense and it is a good way of accessing the path to the profile easily. Look at the following script; it will illustrate the technique for you:

```
PS C:\> $profile

C:\Users\ed.IAMMRED\Documents\WindowsPowerShell\Micro
soft.PowerShell_profile.ps1
```

When you use the PowerShell ISE to query $profile, you will get this output:

```
PS C:\Users\ed.IAMMRED> $profile

C:\Users\ed.IAMMRED\Documents\WindowsPowerShell\Micro
soft.PowerShellISE_profile.ps1
```

To save you from having to try to analyze yourself, there is one difference between PowerShell Console Current User,

Current Host, and PowerShell ISE Current User, Current Host profiles – the letters ISE. Remember that because, if you are attempting to set something in the PowerShell Console Profile, it must be available in the ISE as well.

All of this will become clearer as you work your way through this book.

Chapter 2

Learning the PowerShell Commands

The commands are the whole point of PowerShell; they are how you get it to do what you want. The commands are known as cmdlets, or Command-lets and they are lightweight scripts that each performs a different function. Each cmdlet can only perform a single function and the most commonly used ones are detailed below:

Get-Help

Because Microsoft is aware that PowerShell is such a huge learning curve, they have included perhaps the most important cmdlet of all – `get-help`. This cmdlet will display information about commands and concepts, including other cmdlets, workflows, functions, CIM commands, aliases, scripts, and providers. To use it, if you want to get help for a specific command, type in `Get-Help`, followed by the name of the command, for example, `Get-Help Get-Process`. If you want to see a list of all the help topics, type in `Get-Help *`.

If you want help with conceptual topics, you need to start the command with about, for example, about_Comparison Operators. If you want to see all the conceptual help topics, type in Get-Help about_*. To see a topic, type in Get-Help about_\<name of topic>, for example, Get Help about_Comparison Operators.

If you need help with a PowerShell provider, type in Get-Help and then the name of the provider. For example, if you wanted help with the provider called Certificate, you would type in Get-Help Certificate

As well as typing Get-Help, you can also shorten it to man or help, which will show you one screen at a time, or you can type in \<cmdlet-name\> -? – this is the same as Get-Help but only for Commands.

Get-Command

Get-Command cmdlet will show you all the commands that you can use on your system, including aliases, cmdlets, workflows, functions, scripts, applications, and filters. To use it, simply type in Get-Command * and you will be shown all commands, including those that are not PowerShell files in the Path variable $eny:path – these will be shown in the Application command type.

You can also pull up specific commands by typing in Get-Command followed by the name of the command you want. This will import the module that houses the command, letting you use it right away.

Get-Member

Whenever you are writing a script or you are working on the command line, one of the biggest problems you will face, especially if you are a beginner, is knowing what you can and cannot do. How do you know which methods and properties you can use? The Get-Member cmdlet can help you – simply connect to an object, pipe it to Get-Member and the return will be the methods and the properties in the object. Let's say that you already know `Get-EventLog` will bring up an event log object, all you need to type in is `Get-EventLog -list | Get-Member`. The return will look something like this:

```
Name                                                 MemberType
          Definition
----                                                 ----------
          ----------
add_Disposed                                         Method
          System.Void add_Disposed(EventHandler v...
add_EntryWritten                                     Method
          System.Void add_EntryWritten(EntryWritt...
BeginInit                                            Method
          System.Void BeginInit()
Clear                                                Method
          System.Void Clear()
Close                                                Method
          System.Void Close()
```

Get-ChildItem

`Get-ChildItem` is what you use to list the objects that are in your current location but there is more to it than that. Let's look at an example. If you were to type in `Get-ChildItem`, you would get something like this returned:

```
Directory: Microsoft.Windows
PowerShell.Core\FileSystem::C:\Documents and
Settings\timdlaton

Mode                LastWriteTime             Length
Name
----                -------------             ------ -
---
d----               3/1/2006    9:03 AM
Bluetooth Software
d---s               5/10/2006   8:55 AM           Cookies
d----               5/9/2006    2:09 PM           Desktop
d-r--               5/9/2006    8:22 AM
Favorites
d-r--               5/9/2006    2:24 PM           My
Documents
d-r--               3/1/2006    8:15 AM           Start
Menu
d---s               3/1/2006    3:41 PM
UserData
d----               3/16/2006    3:29 PM          WINDOWS
```

Notice that there isn't really a lot to see here, but that is only because the location only contained a few subfolders. What you really need is for `Get-ChildItem` to give you the subfolder names and the contents of each one. To get that, you would simply add the parameter called `recurse`:

```
Get-ChildItem -recurse
```

There are plenty of other ways that you can use Get-ChildItem and you will learn about those as you work your way through PowerShell.

Using Format Cmdlets

PowerShell also contains a set of Format cmdlets that let you control which properties are shown for specific objects. These cmdlets start with Format and include:

- `Format-Wide`
- `Format-List`
- `Format-Table`
- `Format-Custom`

Each of these cmdlets has default properties that are used if you do not specify other ones. To specify which property you want to be displayed, each cmdlet will use the same parameter of Property. `Format-Wide` only displays a single property do the parameter only has a single value but `Format-Table` and `Format-List` will each accept lists of property names.

Net Objects

.NET objects are created from .NET classes. Objects are instances of classes and methods are the functions that work exclusively on those objects. PowerShell provides built-in support for .NET objects, a way for you to access both instance and static methods and properties. If you wanted to call a static method on a specific class, you would input the name inside of square brackets and then make sure the class name and method name are separated by a pair of colons, as such:

```
[ClassName]::MethodName(parameter list)
```

If you wanted to call a method on a specific object, you would insert a dot between the method name and the variable that is representing the object, as such:

```
$objectReference.MethodName(parameter list)
```

.NET objects allow you to create a new framework to work from, ensuring that you use only the objects that are designed to be associated with the tasks you need them for.

Classes Objects

Classes are blueprints for objects, a model that defines the object structure. Objects contain data that is accessed through a property and that can be worked on using a method. In case you hadn't realized, you have been working with objects ever since you used your very first cmdlet.

When you create an object, you are creating an instance of an object. We call this instantiating and it results in the creation of a new object in memory that is based on a specific class. The example shows you how to create an object that is derived from the class called PSObject, already in PowerShell and this is the way we did it before v5 was released:

```
    $Properties = @{

    "FirstName" = 'Stéphane'

    "LastName" = 'van Gulick'

    "WebSite" = 'www.PowerShelldistrict.com'

}

$Object = New-object -TypeName psobject -Property
$properties

$Object
```

What we have done here is create an object and saved it in the variable called $object. If you look in that variable, you will see that it has all the data listed in a structured way.

In PowerShell 5, we got the ability to create our own classes and this is how we create the exact same object as above but, this time, using our own class:

```
Class Author {

    $FirstName = 'Stéphane'
```

```
    $LastName = 'van Gulick'

    $WebSite = 'www.PowerShelldistrict.Com'

}

New-Object Author
```

Note that you have set the default values for your properties with this code.

Classes can be instantiated in two ways:

```
#Instantiating a class method n°1

    [Author]::new()

#Instantiating a class method n°2

    New-Object Author
```

Both methods provide the same result and the first method is the exact same syntax that is used in C#. When the beta version of PowerShell 5 was released, this was the only way to create an object. Look at the class below; it has 4 properties:

- `Firstname`
- `LastName`
- `UserName`
- `EmployeeType`

Each of these is of the same type – String – and none has any predefined values:

```
Class Employee {

    [string]$FirstName

    [string]$LastName

    [string]$UserName

    [string]$EmployeeType

}
```

The Pipeline

If you really want to get to grips with PowerShell, the most important thing to understand is the PowerShell pipeline. This is a key concept simply because everything that you do in PowerShell happening in the pipeline. To start with, we need to think of the pipeline as a length of pipe. The commands will enter one end and the objects exit at the other. You won't always be able to see what is going on in the pipe but you can give it some direction. The pipe symbol is the vertical bar - | - and this is what tells PowerShell that you want to pass the output of one command as the input of the next. While this is by no means a new concept, in PowerShell, you are passing entire objects rather than just text.

As a simple example, type **Get-Service** at the command prompt. This cmdlet will create all the objects needed to represent all the services that are on your computer and

PowerShell will display the results. Try it now and see what your output is.

The thing is, these are objects, along with the describing properties and PowerShell has the `Sort-Object` command to help you sort them. It does need an object type to sort and, if you look at help, you can see that the parameter called `InputObject` will accept the pipeline input `ByValue`. Put in another way, PowerShell will assume that, if `Sort-Object` detects anything that comes from the pipeline, it also belongs to the parameter and that means you don't need to specify it.

Let's look at an easy example of a PowerShell pipeline.

To keep refining your results until you get what you need, you should use pipelined expressions. For beginners, you should do this in several steps, like this example:

1. First, you must sort all the processes in descending order by Virtual memory:

```
get-process | sort -Property "VirtualMemorySize" -
Descending
```

2. The results will depend on whether the Get-Process command has worked, if not you must run that first. If you get the results you expect, you can move on to the next step:

```
get-process | sort -Property "VirtualMemorySize" -
Descending | Select -first 10
```

3. Continue adding in steps as needed to get the result you want:

```
get-process | sort -property "VirtualMemorySize" -
descending | Select -first 10 | measure-object
VirtualMemorySize -sum -average
```

What you will also learn here is that objects can and do change. We started with process objects but by the time we get to the end of the expression, we have a measurement object. If you don't get what you expect by using a pipelined expression, rerun the command and make sure you pipe the results to the cmdlet called `Get-Member` so that you can identify what comes out of the pipeline. Then get rid of the last bit of the expression and rerun it, making sure that the results are piped to Get-Member.

Tab Complete

One of the more useful features of PowerShell is that the Tab button can be used to complete a line. The Tab Completion button helps you to complete entries in the Command Pane or the Script Pane.

- **Automatically Completing a Command Entry**

In the Script or Command pane, type the first few characters of any command and press the Tab key. If there is only one command that matches the text, it will be automatically completed for you. If there are several commands, all of them will be shown and you can choose the right one by pressing the Tab button repeatedly until the right one is selected. You can use this to complete parameter names, cmdlet names, object property names, variable names or file paths.

- **Automatically Completing a cmdlet Parameter Entry**

From the Script or Command pane, type a cmdlet in and then a dash. Press the Tab key to see the parameters associated with the cmdlet. If there are more than one, press the Tab key repeatedly to see them all.

Chapter 3

PowerShell Script Creation

As you get more used to PowerShell and you begin to understand the advantages of using it, your attention should be turning to writing those all-important scripts. In this chapter, I am going to give you an overview of scripting with some examples that you can input into your own consoles to see how they work. First, a quick reference guide before we get into the nitty gritty.

Creating and Running Scripts

PowerShell files can be opened and edited in the Script Pane and there are specific files – script files end with .ps1, script data files end in .psd1, and script module files end in .ps1xml. You can also open XML, configuration and text files in the pane.

Creating a New Script File

Open PowerShell and click on **New** on the toolbar or in the **File** menu. A newly created file will now show up under the current PowerShell tab in a new file tab. The file will be saved as .ps1 by default but you can give it a new name and save it with a different extension if you wish. You can create multiple files in one PowerShell tab.

Opening an Existing Script

Click on **Open** in the **File** menu or on the toolbar. In the dialog box, click the file you want and it will appear in a new tab

Closing a Script Tab

Click the script tab on the one you want closing and then either click the X in the corner of the tab or click on **File>Close.** If you changed the file since it was last saved, you will need to save or discard the changes

Displaying the File Path

Go to the File tab and hover the mouse over the file name – you will see a tooltip appear with the file path displayed

Running a Script

Click on **Run Script** on the toolbar or **File>Run**

Running Part of a Script

Choose the portion of script you want to run from the script pane and then click on **Run Selection** or **File>Run Selection**

Stopping a Script

Click on **Stop Operation** on the toolbar, or **File>Stop Operation** or you can press the CTRL+BREAK keys on your keyboard. If you have no text selected, you can also use CTRL+C. If text is selected, using CTRL+C will map to the copy function

Writing and Editing in the Script Pane

The following steps will show you how to edit text. You can do the following:

- Cut
- Copy
- Paste
- Find
- Replace
- Undo or redo the last action

To Enter Text into the Script Pane:

1. Click anywhere in the script pane or click on **View>Go to Script Pane**
2. Create your script

To Find Text in the Pane:

1. Press on **CTRL+F** or click **Edit>Find in Script** to find text anywhere in the script
2. To find text that is after the cursor, press **SHIFT+F3** or click n **Edit>Find Next in Script**

3. To find text that is before the cursor, press **SHIFT+F3** or click on **Edit>Find Previous in Script**

To Replace Text in the Script Pane:

Press on **CTRL+H** or click on **Edit>Replace in Script.** Now type in the text you are looking for and the text you want to replace it with and hit Enter.

Finding a Specific Line in the Script Pane:

While in the Script Pane, click on **Edit>Go to Line** or press **CTRL+G** and then type in the line number

Cutting Text:

1. While in the Script Pane, select the portion of text to be cut
2. Press **CTRL+X**, or click the **Cut** icon on the toolbar or click on **Edit>Cut**

Copying Text:

1. Choose the text that you want copying in the Script Pane
2. Click **Edit>Copy,** or the **Cut** icon on the toolbar or press on **CTRL+C**

Pasting Text:

Click on the **Paste** icon n the toolbar, click on **Edit>Paste** or press **CTRL+V**

Undoing an Action:

Click on the **Undo** icon on the toolbar, or click on **Edit>Undo** or press on **Ctrl+Z**

Redoing an Action:

Click on **Edit>Redo**, or click the **Redo** icon on the toolbar or press on **CTRL+Y**

How to Save Scripts

These steps will show you how to name and save your scripts. A file that has not been saved since alteration will display an asterisk beside the name; this disappears when you save the file.

Saving a Script:

Click on **File>Save,** or click the **Save** icon on the toolbar or press **CTRL+S**

Saving and Naming:

1. Click on **File>Save As**
2. In the dialog box type a name in the **File Name** box
3. Select the file type from the **Save as Type** box
4. Click on **Save**

Saving Scripts in ASCII Encoding

Windows PowerShell ISE is set, by default, to save any new script, script data or script module files as Unicode. If you wanted to save as ASCII, or any other type of encoding, use the Save As method on $`psISE.CurrentFile` object. The command below is used to save new scripts as MyScript.ps1 but with ASCII encoding:

```
$psise.CurrentFile.SaveAs("MyScript.ps1",
[System.Text.Encoding]::ASCII)
```

The next command will replace a current script file with one of the same name but which has ASCII encoding:

```
$psise.CurrentFile.Save([System.Text.Encoding]::ASCII
)
```

This command will tell you the encoding of your current file:

```
$psise.CurrentFile.encoding
```

PowerShell Script Files

Follow the examples given in this chapter, type then into your own ISE but make sure you begin on line 1 – that way everything will match up as it should.

All a PowerShell script file is, is a text file with a .ps1 extension. It isn't exactly a command-line batch file and running your script isn't going to be quite the same as running those commands yourself. Let me demonstrate that. Open a console window, type the following in and run it, remembering to press Enter after each code line (don't type in the line numbers!)

```
T-SQL

Get-Service

Get-Process
```

Now type that into the ISE Script editing pane and run it. Each one will give you a different result. In Windows PowerShell whenever you hit Enter, you begin a new pipeline and whatever is typed in will run in that pipeline. At the end, PowerShell will convert it to a text display. Running both commands in the normal console results in two separate pipelines. However, when you run them in ISE, both commands go into one pipeline. Try this command:

```
T-SQL

Get-Service;Get-Process
```

The results should look the same as they did when you ran the script.

What I am trying to demonstrate is that scripts should only produces a single type of output and the last thing you want is a script dropping several different types of command into one pipeline at the same time. Keep that in mind as a rule from now on: the only time it will be different is if a script is used for several functions, in which case, each one should have just one output type.

Variables

Variables are containers where you can store things, whether they are of the same type or not. The box is given a name but, when you choose your name stick to using letters, underscores and numbers – not spaces. The name will reference the whole box but, if you wanted to reference what was stored in the box, you would add a $ to the front of the name – the sign does not become a part of the name, it is merely a pointer for PowerShell that you don't want the box, you want what is inside it. Look at these examples:

```
T-SQL

$var = 'hello'

$number = 1

$numbers = 1,2,3,4,5,6,7,8,9
```

These show you how to use the assignment operator (=) to put items into variables. The last example will create an array because all lists that are separated by commas are seen as arrays or collections. The first example is assigning a string object with the characters in between the quotation marks being the ones in the string.

There is one thing in PowerShell that can be confusing to a newcomer – PowerShell will not understand a meaning that is associated with a variable name; for example, $computername will not tell PowerShell that there is a computer name in the variable. In the same way, $numbers will not tell PowerShell that there is more than 1 number in a variable. It matters not whether you use a plural for your name. Look at this example:

```
T-SQL

$numbers = 1
```

Is as valid to PowerShell as the next one is:

```
T-SQL

$numbers = 'bill.'
```

When there are multiple values in a variable, there is a specific syntax to use if you wanted to access one value:

- $numbers[0] as the first,
- $numbers[1] as the second,
- $numbers[-1] as the last,
- $numbers[-2] as the second-last and so on.

Quotation Marks

Use single quotation marks for delimiting variables unless there is a good reason to do otherwise. There are three times when you might want to use double quotes:

1. When the contents of a variable are inserted into a string. Inside the double quotes, PowerShell looks for the $ and assumes that everything after it, up to the first illegal character, is a variable name. The variable contents will then replace the $ and the variable name:

```
T-SQL

$name = Andy

$prompt = "My name is $name"
```

$prompt will now have the name "My name is Andy", because $name has been replaced with the contents of the variable. This is a good way to join strings without concatenating them.

2. With the Backtick, escape character or gave accent PowerShell will look for these inside double quotes and do what is necessary. Look at these examples:

```
T-SQL

$debug = "`$computer contains $computer"

$head = "Column`tColumn`tColumn"
```

In the first one, the initial $ is escaped which removes the special meaning it has as a variable accessor.

In the second one, `t is representing a horizontal tab character. PowerShell puts a tab in between each Column.

3. When single quotes are needed in a string

```
T-SQL

$filter1 = "name='BITS'"

$computer = 'BITS'

$filter2 = "name='$computer'"
```

The literal string is called name=BITS and the whole name is enclosed in double quotes. $filter1 and $filter2 now contain the same things but $filter2 got there using the double quotes. Do note, it is only the outermost quotes that count and PowerShell will ignore the single quotes in the string.

Object Members and Variables

Everything in PowerShell is an object, even a basic string. Any object can be piped to Get-Member to show the name of the object type and the members, including methods and properties:

```
T-SQL

$var = 'Hello'

$var | Get-Member
```

If you don't want PowerShell to access the whole object in the variable, put a period after the name of the variable. This also tells PowerShell that you just want one method or property accessed. Follow the period with the name of that method or property.

A method name must always be followed by parentheses. Some will accept an input argument and these augments go inside the parentheses, in a list separated by commas. Other methods don't need any arguments but the parentheses are still required; they will be empty:

```
T-SQL

$svc = Get-Service

$svc[0].name

$name = $svc[1].name

$name.length

$name.ToUpper()
```

Look at the second line; the first thing it does is access the first item inside $svc. The period is telling PowerShell that it only wants to access one property or method, in this case the name property. The fifth line shows you how to access a method by putting the name after the period and then the obligatory parentheses.

Normally, a period would be considered an illegal character in the name of a variable and, as such, the second line in the next example isn't going to work the way you think it will:

```
T-SQL

$service = 'bits'

$name = "Service is $service.ToUpper()"

$upper = $name.ToUpper()

$name = "Service is $upper"
```

On the second line, $name contains "Service is BITS.ToUPPER()" while, on the fourth line, it contains "Service is BITS."

Parentheses

As well as being used with object methods, parentheses are also used to denote the order of execution for PowerShell. In other words, the parentheses denote to PowerShell that this should be executed first. The whole parenthetical expression would be replaced by the result of the expression. Look at this example, have a go at it and see if you can get your head around it:

```
T-SQL

$name = (Get-Service)[0].name

Get-Service -computerName (Get-Content names.txt)
```

On the first line, $name contains the name of the first service that is on the system. To read this, start with the parenthetical expression as that is what PowerShell will begin with. Get-Service resolves to an array of services. The [0] is accessing the first item in the array, hence it being the first service. As it is followed by the period, we know that we are going to access a method or a property, rather than the whole object. Lastly, we can pull just the service name out.

On the second line, the parenthetical expression reads a text file's contents. Assuming that the file has one computer name on each line, Get-Content can then return a collection, or array, of those computer names. These are given to the Get-Service parameter called "-computerName". Because the parameter can accept string arrays, any parenthetical expression that will return string arrays can be given to it.

PowerShell Scripting Language

Compared to full programming languages, PowerShell is very simple, containing less than 24 keywords. However, although it is simple, it is more than enough to do the job it was designed for and, although it would take me forever to go over everything, I am going to give you an overview of the major constructs. Don't forget that you can use "about ..." to get help on a certain topic or you can use "about**" to get a whole list of help topics.

The If Construct

This is the decision-making construct and, in its fullest form, looks like this:

```
T-SQL

If ($this -eq $that) {

  # commands

} elseif ($those -ne $them) {

  # commands

} elseif ($we -gt $they) {

  # commands

} else {

  # commands

}
```

The “if” keyword is mandatory in the construct and, following that, is a parenthetical expression that must evaluate True or False. PowerShell interprets nonzero as True and zero as false.

PowerShell will also recognize $true and $false, built-in variables, as representing the Boolean values. If the parenthetical expression is True, the command that are inside the curly brackets will be executed, if it is False, they won’t.

The elseif construct works in pretty much the same way; it gets its own parenthetical expression and must evaluate to

True or False. The else block will only be executed if none of the blocks before it executes.

is a comment character and PowerShell will ignore anything between that and the carriage return. Notice how carefully the constructs in the above example were formatted; you might also see something like this:

```
T-SQL

if ($those -eq $these)

{

  #commands

}
```

Where the curly brackets are placed is not important; what matters is that your placement is consistent. That goes for indentation as well – every line inside a curly bracket set must be indented the same. That's where the TAB key comes in, defaulting to an indent of four characters. Indentation is a core practice you need to get the hang of; if you don't, you won't be able to match open and closed curly brackets in the more complex scripts. Look at this example of a script that has been badly formatted:

```
T-SQL

function mine {

if ($this -eq $that){
```

```
get-service

}}
```

Can you see how much harder it is to read, to maintain, troubleshoot and debug? It isn't necessary to add a space after closing parentheses but it is easier to read. This is much better:

```
T-SQL

function mine {

 if ($this -eq $that){

  get-service

 }

}
```

Although you don't need to put that closing parentheses on its own, it does make the code look better. Learn to format neatly and you won't have so many scripting problems.

The Do While Construct

This is a looping construct and is used to repeat command blocks, so long as a condition is True or until it becomes True. Here's how it is used:

```
T-SQL

Do {
```

```
  # commands
} While ($this -eq $that)
```

The commands inside the curly brackets will execute at least once. The While condition doesn't get evaluated until the first execution has happened. You can move the While condition but the commands will then execute only if the condition is True to start with:

```
T-SQL
While (Test-Path $path) {
  # commands
}
```

The second example doesn't have any comparison operator in it and that is because the cmdlet called Test-Path already returns True or False so there is no need to compare it with True or False.

The parenthetical expression that is used with the constructs only needs to do one thing – simplify to True or False. If you use Test-Path, or another command that will always return True or False, you don't need anything else.

The ForEach Construct

This is like the cmdlet called ForEach, differing only in syntax. The purpose of this is to enumerate the objects within a specific array so that you can work on them one at a time:

```
T-SQL

$services = Get-Service

ForEach ($service in $services) {

  $service.Stop()

}
```

Don't overthink this; just keep it in mind that the plural words mean nothing to PowerShell. The name is purely to remind you that there are one or more services in it, nothing more.

The "in" keyword that you see on the second line is part of the syntax of ForEach and the $service variable is just a made-up name.

PowerShell repeats the commands in the construct (this in the curly brackets) once for each of the objects that are in the second variable. Each time, it takes one object from the second variable and puts it into the first variable.

Other Constructs

There are other constructs in PowerShell and you can get all the information you need from the built-in help topics. On occasion, you can use the constructs above to replace any of the others. For example, you could use an If construct with several elseif sections instead of Switch, or you can use ForEach construct or ForEach-Object cmdlet instead of For. For example, if you have a script that contains a loop that you want to execute 10 times:

```
T-SQL

1..10 | ForEach-Object -process {

  # code here will repeat 10 times

  # use $_ to access the current iteration

  # number

}
```

Really, all you need to do is pick the best construct for the job.

Functions

Functions are special construct types, used to contain groups of commands that are related and that all perform one specific task. In general, you could take any Script in PowerShell and wrap it up in a function:

```
T-SQL

function Mine {

  Get-Service
```

```
  Get-Process
}
```

Mine

Look at line five – a new function has been defined, effectively turning Mine into a command. This means you can just enter the name to run the function and that is what is happening in line five. Functions are usually contained in a script file and one script can have multiple functions; you can even have a function within a function.

Adding Parameters to a Script

It is highly unlikely that you will create a script that does the same thing each time you run it. More often than not, your scripts will contain variable behavior or variable data and these variations can be helped along with parameters.

Parameters are always defined at the top of a script and they are defined in special ways. This definition can be preceded with comments but it must always be the first line or lines of code to be executed. Each parameter is separated by a comma and it helps if you can place each parameter on its own line. Look at this example:

```
T-SQL
param (
  [string]$computername,
```

```
    [string]$logfile,

    [int]$attemptcount = 5

)
```

There are three parameters defined here and, inside of the script, they are used the same way as any variable. On line four, a default value has been assigned to $attemptcount; if there are any input parameters, these will override the default but, if the parameter is not specified when the script is run, the default will be used. The following shows a few ways the script can be run, assuming that it has been saved as Test.ps1:

```
T-SQL

./test -computername SERVER

./test -comp SERVER -log err.txt -attempt 2

./test SERVER err.txt 2

./test SERVER 2

./test -log err.txt -attempt 2 -comp SERVER
```

Parameters are accepted by the script in pretty much the same way as any cmdlet. Variable names have been used as the parameter names, with the dash that goes in front of all parameter names and here's how that code works:

- Line one – just one parameter specified, meaning $logfile is empty and $attemptcount contains the default 5
- Line two – all three parameters specified with shortened names.
- Line three – all three parameters displayed positionally, with no names. Just remember to provide the right values in the right order
- Line four – this is what will happen if you don't take care! $computername contains 'SERVER" and $logfile contains 2, while $attemptcount has 5. That is not what was intended and is what can happen if you don't use parameter names.
- Line five - much better. The parameters are not specified in order but, because the names have been used, it doesn't matter.

Chapter 4

PowerShell Providers

PowerShell providers allow you to see your data stores as if they were file systems on a mounted drive. For example, the Registry provider, already built-in to PowerShell lets you navigate through the registry as if you were navigating the hard drive on your computer. Providers are also able to override the Item cmdlets, like Set-Item, Get-Item, etc., in such a way that the data that is in your data stores can be treated in the same way that you treat files and directories when you look through a file system.

Understanding Providers

The PowerShell providers define the logic that needs to be used for accessing, navigating and editing the data stores and the drive will specify the point of entry to the data store, which is of a type defined by the provider. For example, the Registry provider gives you access to keys and hives in a registry and the drives HKCU and HKLM specify which hives are to be accessed in the registry.

When you write providers, you specify the default drives – those that are automatically created when the specific provider is available – and you also define the methods used to create new drives which use the provider.

Type of Providers

There are a number of provider types, each of which has a different function level. Providers are implemented in classes that are derived from a descendant of the cmdletProvider class.

Provider Cmdlets

Providers are able to implement methods that correspond to certain cmdlets. They create custom behaviors for each cmdlet for when it is used in a drive for the specific provider. Depending on the provider type, there are different cmdlet sets available.

Provider Paths

Because you can navigate a provider drive like you would a file system, you would expect the syntax of the provider paths to match the paths that you use in file navigation. When you run a provider cmdlet, you specify which path is to be used to access the item and that path can then be interpreted in several ways. Each provider should support at least one of the following types of path:

- **Drive-Qualified Paths**

This is a combination of the name of the item, the container and the sub container/s where the item is located and of the PowerShell drive that the item is accessed through. The drive is defined by the provider being used to access the data store and the path should start with name of the drive, followed by a coon, for example, get-childitem C:

- **Provider-Qualified Paths**

For PowerShell to both initialize and then uninitialize the provider, that provider must have support for a provider-qualified path. For example, with the FileSystem provider, you can initialize and then uninitialize it because it defines a provider-qualified path – FileSystem::\\uncshare\abc\bar

- **Provider-Direct Paths**

If you want to remotely access your PowerShell provider, that provider has to support a provider-direct path that will pass straight to the provider for the current location. For example, the Registry provider uses \\server\regkeypath as its provider-direct path

- **Provider-Internal Paths**

To give the provider cmdlet access to data through APIs (Application Programing Interfaces), the PowerShell provider must support a provider-internal path. This is indicated in the provider-qualified path after the ::. For example, the PowerShell FileSystem provider has a provider-internal path of \\uncshare\abc\bar.

Dynamic Parameters

Providers are able to define some dynamic parameters that will be added to a provider cmdlet when a user has specified a value for a static parameter of said cmdlet. This is done by the provider implementing at least one dynamic parameter method.

Provider Capabilities

There are several capabilities that providers are able to support and these are defined by the ProviderCapabilities enumeration. These capabilities include being able to use wildcards, support transactions and filter items. If you want to specify the capabilities for a specific provider, you need to add a list of the values for the ProviderCapabilities enumeration, combine these with a logical OR operation, as the property of the ProviderCapabilities, which is parameter 2 of the attribute, of the cmdletProviderAttribute for the provider class. For example, the attribute below specifies that the provider has support for the Transactions and ShouldProcess capabilities:

```
[CmdletProvider(RegistryProvider.ProviderName,
ProviderCapabilities.ShouldProcess                    |
ProviderCapabilities.Transactions)]
```

Provider Cmdlet Help

When you write a provider, you can implement Help for the provider cmdlets that you are supporting. This will include a help topic for each of the individual cmdlets or multiple help topic versions for when the cmdlets act differently according to how the dynamic parameters are used. To support the cmdlet-specific help, the provider has got to implement ICmdletProviderSupportsHelp interface.

To display the Help topic for each of the provider cmdlets, PowerShell calls the method GetHelpMaml. The PowerShell engine provides the cmdlet name that the user had already specified when the Get-Help cmdlet was run, along with the user's current path. This path is necessary if the provider can implement several different versions of a provider cmdlet for several different drives. The method has to return a string that has the cmdlet Help XML in it.

The Help file content is written with PSMAML XML, the same schema that is used when the standalone cmdlet Help content is written. The content for a custom Help cmdlet can be added to the Help file for the provider, underneath the element called CmdletsHelpPaths. The next example shows you the element for a single provider cmdlet and how to specify the provider cmdlet name that is supported by the provider:

```
<CmdletHelpPaths>
  <command:command>
    <command:details>
      <command:name>ProviderCmdletName</command:name>
      <command:verb>Verb</command:verb>
      <command:noun>Noun</command:noun>
    <command:details>
  </command:command>
<CmdletHelpPath>
```

The File System

The FileSystem Providers in PowerShell allow you to change, add, delete and clear directories and files from PowerShell. It lets you see the PowerShell drives that correspond logically to drives on your computer, including those that have been mapped to network shares. Thus, you can reference all of these drives from inside PowerShell and refer to folders or files in the same way that you would refer to them in your Windows operating system.

To refer to a drive, you need to specify the name of the drive, followed with a colon. Like most of PowerShell, the FileSystem provider isn't case sensitive and, as such, you can use C: or c: to get the folders and files from the C drive.

For the name to be fully qualified, it must be in the following format order:

- The name of the drive
- A colon
- The names of any directories or subdirectories
- The file name, if applicable

Each of the elements that make up a fully qualified name must be separated by a forward (/) slash OR a backslash (\). Look at the following example of Shell.dll. This files are on C: drive, in the system32 subdirectory of Windows directory:

```
C:\Windows\System32\shell.dll
```

If there are spaces in any of the elements in a fully qualified name, the name must be enclosed in quote marks, for example:

```
"C:\Program Files\Internet Explorer\iexplore.exe"
```

The period (.) represents that current location in the file system.

For example, let's say that the current location is C:\Windows\System32. You would then refer to the Shell.dll file within that directory as such:

```
.\Shell.dll
```

If you want to use the FileSystem provider to manage and view folders and files, you would use the provider cmdlets, like Set-Location (cd) or Get-ChildItem (dir, ls). PowerShell also has a function called mkdir (md) that makes use of the New-Item cmdlet to let you create new directories.

The Alias

The PowerShell Alias provider allows you to add, get, clear, change and delete aliases from PowerShell. The alias is the alternative name for a function, cmdlet or an executable file. PowerShell has its own built-in aliases but you are able to add your own to a current session or you can add them to your PowerShell profile.

The Alias provider contains just alias objects and is a flat namespace; none of them have any child items. Each one is an instance of the class called System.Management.Automation.AliasInfo.

The Alias provider will show its data store in the Alias: drive. To work with an alias, you can use the following command to change your current location to the Alias: drive:

```
Set-Location alias:
```

You can also work from any other drive in PowerShell; simple add the Alias: drive name to the path when you want to reference it from another location.

PowerShell has a group of cmdlets that are designed to change or view aliases:

- Set-Alias
- New-Alias
- Import-Alias
- Get-Alias
- Export-Alias

If you are using these, there is no need to specify Alias: drive in the name.

The Function

The PowerShell Function provider allows you to add, get, change, delete and clear filters and functions in PowerShell. Functions are named blocks of code that each perform a specific action. When the function name is typed in, the code that is within the function will run. Filters are named blocks of code that are responsible for establishing a set of conditions for a specific action. Filter names can be type in place of a condition, as in the command, Where-Object.

Within the Function: drive, each function name is preceded by the “function” label, while filters have the preceding label of “filter”. Irrespective of the labels, provided they are used in the right context, they will operate as they should do.

The Function provider contains only filter and function objects and is a flat namespace; neither the filters nor the functions have child items.

Each function is an instance of the class named System.Management.Automation.FunctionInfo and each filter is an instance of the class named System.Management.Automation.FilterInfo.

The data store for the Function provider is exposed in the Function: drive and, to work with these functions your location can be changed to the Function: drive (set-location function). If you want to reference a function from another location, such as another PowerShell drive, you should use the Function: name in the path.

The Function provider has support for all cmdlets with a name containing the noun Item (the Item cmdlets), with the exception of Invoke-Item. It also has support for the cmdlets Set-Content and Get-Content. It does not support any cmdlet that has a name containing the ItemProperty noun and it has no support for the Filter parameter in any of the cmdlets.

All changes to the functions affect the current console only. To save the changes, add the function to the Windows PowerShell profile, or use Export-Console to save the current console.

The Environment

The PowerShell Environment provider allows you to change, add, get, delete and clear environment variables from PowerShell. The Environment provider contains only those objects that are representative of environment variables and is a flat namespace; the variables do not have any child items.

Each of the environment variables is an instance of the class called System.Collections.DictionaryEntry. The variable name is the dictionary key and the environment variable value is the dictionary value.

The data store of the Environment provider is exposed in the Env: drive and, to work with the variables, your current location should be changed to Env: drive (set-location env:) or, you can work from another location such as another PowerShell drive and referencing the environment variable from that location is done by using Env: drive name in the path.

The Environment provider has support for all cmdlets that contain the noun Item, with the exception of the Invoke-Item cmdlet and it also provides support for the Set-Content and Get-Content cmdlets. It does not have any support for cmdlets with the noun ItemProperty nor for the Filter parameter in any of the cmdlets.

Environment variables have to conform to the normal variable naming standards and there cannot be an = in the name. If you make changes to the environment variable, they will only affect the current session; if you want those changes to be saved, you must add them to PowerShell profile or save the current session using Export-Console.

The Registry

The PowerShell Registry Provider allows you to add, get, change, delete and clear entries, values and keys in the registry through PowerShell. The keys are instances of the class called Microsoft.Win32.RegistryKey and entries are instances of the class called PSCustomObject.

The Registry provider allows you access to a hierarchical namespace made up of keys and subkeys. The entries and the values are not included in that hierarchy; instead, they are properties of individual keys.

The Registry provider has support for all cmdlets that have the Item noun (Item cmdlets), like Copy-Item, Get-Item, and Rename-Item. The only exception is Invoke-Item, which is not supported. You should always use these Item cmdlets whenever you are working with the registry keys and subkeys. This provider also has support for cmdlets that have the ItemProperty noun and the ItemProperty cmdlet should always be used whenever you work with the registry entries.

You are not able to use any cmdlets that have the Content noun with this provider.

Each of the individual Registry keys is protected with a security descriptor and, to see that descriptor, you can use Get-Acl.

The Certificate

The PowerShell Certificate provider allows you to navigate through the certificate namespace and see the certificates and certificate stores. You can also use it to open the Certificates snapin for MMC – the Microsoft Management Console.

Note - From PowerShell 3 onwards, the Microsoft.PowerShell.Security module, home to the Certificate Provider, will not be automatically imported into each session. To use it, you need to use Cert: drive and either use the cmdlet called Import-Module or run a command that makes use of the Cert: drive, like Set-Location Cert:

It is also worth noting that, from v3 onwards, the Certificate provider also has much better support the management of SSL – Secure Socket Layer – certificates for web hosting. This is done through the addition of support for dynamic parameters and cmdlets that both create and delete certificate stores that are located in LocalMachine and for finding, moving and deleting certificates.

There are also several new dynamic parameters in the Get-ChildItem cmdlet in Cert: including:

- DnsName
- EKU
- SSLServerAuthentication
- ExpiringInDays

A new dynamic parameter called DeleteKey has been included in Remove-Item in Cert: These are all available in PowerShell 3 and higher and all work with IIS 8.0, on Windows Server 2012, up to and including Windows 10.

There are some new script properties added to X509Certificate2 object, including:

- DnsNameList
- EnhancedKeyUsageList
- SendAsTrustedIssuer

These all make it much easier to both find and to manage certificates.

All of these new features allow you to use DNS names and expiration dates to search for certificates and to distinguish between server and client certificates based on the EKU – Enhanced Key Usage – properties.

If all of that weren't enough, the PowerShell Security Module – Microsoft.PowerShell.Security – also now has cmdlets to get certificates ad to both get and set Authenticode signatures. To see all of the cmdlets included in the Security module, just type Get-Command -module *security.

Chapter 5

Working with Files and Folders

You can easily navigate the PowerShell drives and manipulate items on the drives in much the same way as you navigate your own file system on your computer hard drive. In this chapter, we are going to look at how you can manipulate the items:

Listing All Files and Folders that are in a Folder

By using the Get-ChildItem cmdlet, you can get all of the items that are in a folder. If you add in an optional Force parameter, you can also display hidden items and system items. For example, the following snippet of code is a command that will display the contents of the PowerShell Drive C:, which has exactly the same in it as the physical C: drive on your computer.

```
Get-ChildItem -Force C:\
```

This command will only list the items contained directly in the drive, pretty much the same as it would if you ran the DIR command, Cmd.exe in Windows or the ls command in a UNIX shell. If you want to see the items that are contained within each of the direct items, you would need to use the -Recurse parameter in your command. Be aware, this can take a very long time to execute, depending on what you have on your computer! To show everything that is on your C; drive, use this command:

```
Get-ChildItem -Force C:\ -Recurse
```

The Get-ChildItem cmdlet is able to filter items using the built-in Filter, Path, Exclude and Include parameters but these tend to be based mainly on Name. You can perform more in-depth filtering on other item properties by using the Where-Object.

Get-ChildItem can filter items with its Path, Filter, Include, and Exclude parameters, but those are typically based only on name. You can perform complex filtering based on other properties of items by using Where-Object. The next code example will find all of the executable files on your C: drive that are in the Program Files folder, between 1 MB and 10 MB in size and that were modified last after December 1, 2016:

```
Get-ChildItem -Path $env:ProgramFiles -Recurse -
Include *.exe | Where-Object -FilterScript
{($_.LastWriteTime -gt "2016-12-01") -and ($_.Length
-ge 1m) -and ($_.Length -le 10m)}
```

Copying Files and Folders

To copy a file or folder, use the Copy-Item Cmdlet The next command will back C:\boot.ini up to C:\boot.bak:

```
Copy-Item -Path c:\boot.ini -Destination c:\boot.bak
```

If that destination is already in existence, the attempt to copy will fail. If you want to over-write a destination that already exists, you should use the Force parameter, as in the example:

```
Copy-Item -Path c:\boot.ini -Destination c:\boot.bak
-Force
```

This will work even if the destination were a read-only destination.

Copying a folder works in much the same way. The next command will copy the C:\temp\test1 folder recursively to the new folder called C:\temp\DeleteMe:

```
Copy-Item C:\temp\test1 -Recurse c:\temp\DeleteMe
```

You can copy selections of items as well. The next command will copy all of the .txt files that are found anywhere within C:\data to C:\temp\text:

```
Copy-Item -Filter *.txt -Path c:\data -Recurse -
Destination c:\temp\text
```

There are also other tools that you can use for copying file system items and Com, ROBOCOPY and XCOPY objects, like Scripting.FileSystemObject, will all work in PowerShell. For example, you could use Scripting.FileSystem, which is a Script Hosting COM class to back C:\boot.ini up to C:\boot.bak:

```
(New-Object -ComObject
Scripting.FileSystemObject).CopyFile("c:\boot.ini",
"c:\boot.bak")
```

Creating Files and Folders

Creating new folders and files works in exactly the same way no matter which PowerShell Provider you use. If the provider has more than one item type in it, for example, the FileSystem provider will distinguish between a folder and a file, you will need to specify which type of item you want. The following command will create a new folder called C:\temp\New Folder:

```
New-Item -Path 'C:\temp\New Folder' -ItemType
"directory"
```

The next command will create a new file that is empty, called C:\temp\New Folder\file.txt:

```
New-Item -Path 'C:\temp\New Folder\file.txt' -
ItemType "file"
```

Removing All of The Files and Folders That are in a Folder

You may also remove contained items by using the Remove-Item cmdlet but, if the item contains anything else in it, you will need to confirm the removal. For example, if you tried to delete C:\temp\DeleteMe, which contains other items, PowerShell will ask you to confirm the deletion before it will do it:

```
Remove-Item C:\temp\DeleteMe

Confirm

The item at C:\temp\DeleteMe has children and the -
recurse parameter was not

specified. If you continue, all children will be
removed with the item. Are you

sure you want to continue?

[Y] Yes  [A] Yes to All  [N] No  [L] No to All  [S]
Suspend  [?] Help

(default is "Y"):
```

You should use the recursive parameter if you are certain that you want to delete everything and you don't want a confirmation prompt for each of the contained items:

```
Remove-Item C:\temp\DeleteMe -Recurse
```

Mapping a Local Folder as a Windows Accessible Drive

Another thing you can do is map a local folder by using the command, subst. The next example shows you the command to create a local drive, P:, that is rooted in the Program Files directory, which is local:

```
subst p: $env:programfiles
```

Just as they are with network drives, any drive that is mapped in PowerShell with the command subst will immediately be visible to the PowerShell shell.

Reading a Text File into an Array

One of the most common formats of storage for text data is a file that contains separate lines, each treated as an individual element. To read a whole file in one go, we would use the Get-Content cmdlet, as in this example:

```
PS> Get-Content -Path C:\boot.ini

[boot loader]
```

```
timeout=5

default=multi(0)disk(0)rdisk(0)partition(1)\WINDOWS

[operating systems]

multi(0)disk(0)rdisk(0)partition(1)\WINDOWS="Microsof
t Windows XP Professional"

 /noexecute=AlwaysOff /fastdetect

multi(0)disk(0)rdisk(0)partition(1)\WINDOWS="
Microsoft Windows XP Professional

with Data Execution Prevention" /noexecute=optin
/fastdetect
```

The Get-Content cmdlet will treat the data that is read from the file as an array, with one element on each line of the file content. This can be confirmed by checking how long the returned content is:

```
PS> (Get-Content -Path C:\boot.ini).Length

6
```

This is one of the most useful commands for putting information lists straight into PowerShell. For example, you might want to store a list of IP addresses or computer names in a file called C:\temp\domainMembers.txt, putting an individual name on each text line. You can then retrieve the contents of that file using Get-Content and place them into a variable called $Computers:

```
$Computers = Get-Content -Path
C:\temp\DomainMembers.txt
```

We now have an array file, with one name in each element, called $Computers.

Output to HTML

You can use the ConvertTo-Html cmdlet to convert a .NET Framework object to HTML for displaying on a Web Browser This cmdlet will display a command output on a web page. You can use the parameters of ConvertTo-Html to:

- Select object properties
- Specify a table format
- Specify a list format
- Specify the HTML page file
- To add text before and/or after an object
- To return just a table or a list fragment and not a strict DTD page

When multiple objects are submitted to the ConvertTo-Html cmdlet, PowerShell will create a list or table based on the properties that are in the first object submitted. If the rest of the objects do not contain any of the properties specified, the property value of that specific object will be an empty cell. If any of the remaining objects do have any additional properties, the property value will not be included in this file. Let's look at a few examples:

Example 1: Create a web page that displays the date

```
PS C:\> ConvertTo-Html -InputObject (Get-Date)
```

This command will create an HTML page that will display the current date properties. The InputObject parameter is used to submit the results of the command Get-Date to the cmdlet called ConvertTo-Html.

Example 2: Create a web page that displays PowerShell aliases

```
PS C:\> Get-Alias | ConvertTo-Html > aliases.htm

PS C:\> Invoke-Item aliases.htm
```

This command will create an HTML page that will list all the PowerShell aliases that are in the current console. The Get-Alias cmdlet is used to fetch the aliases and the pipeline operator is used to send those aliases to the ConvertTo-Html cmdlet, which will then create the HTML page.

Output to XML

The cmdlet called ConvertTo-XML will create a representation of one or more objects from the .NET Framework. These representations will be XML-based. To use the ConvertTo-XML cmdlet, you must pipe at least one object to it or you must specify the object by using the InputObject parameter.

When several objects are piped to ConvertTo-XML, or the InputObject parameter is used to submit several objects, the ConvertTo-XML cmdlet will return one XML document that lists all representations of all objects.

The ConvertTo-XML cmdlet is similar to the Export-Clixml cmdlet except that the latter will store the XML in a file, while ConvertTo-XML will return the XML so that you can continue processing it in PowerShell. Let's look at a couple of examples:

Example 1: Convert a date into XML

```
PS C:\> Get-Date | ConvertTo-Xml
```

This command will convert the current date, which is a DateTime object, into XML.

Example 2: Convert processes into XML

```
PS C:\> ConvertTo-Xml -As "Document" -InputObject
(Get-Process) -Depth 3
```

This command will convert process objects, those that represent all processes on your computer, into an XML document. These objects will be expanded to three levels.

Working with CSV

CSV files are simple formats that contain tabular data, like an Excel spreadsheet. There are two ways of working with these files.

Export or Convert

The ConvertTo-CSV cmdlet will return a series of strings, each separated by commas, that are representative of the objects you submit. Then you use the ConvertFrom-CSV cmdlet to re-create the objects from the CSV strings. The objects that result from this are CSV versions of the original objects, containing no methods but they do contain string representations of each of the property values.

You could also use the cmdlets called T:Microsoft:PowerShell.Commands.Import-CSV and T:Microsoft.PowerShell.Commands.Export-CSV to convert an object to a CSV string and vice versa. The only difference between ConvertTo-CSV and Export-CSV is that the former will save the CSV strings into a file.

The parameters of the ConvertTo-CSV cmdlet can be used to specify a delimiter that is not a comma or to tell ConvertTo-CSV that the default delimiter should be used to for the current culture. A couple of examples:

Example 1

```
PS C:\> get-process powershell | convertto-csv
```

```
#TYPE System.Diagnostics.Process

"__NounName","Name","Handles","VM","WS","PM","NPM","P
ath","Company","CPU","FileVersion","ProductVersion","
Description",

"Product","BasePriority","ExitCode","HasExited","Exit
Time","Handle","HandleCount","Id","MachineName","Main
WindowHandle"

,"MainWindowTitle","MainModule","MaxWorkingSet","MinW
orkingSet","Modules","NonpagedSystemMemorySize","Nonp
agedSystemMem

orySize64","PagedMemorySize","PagedMemorySize64","Pag
edSystemMemorySize","PagedSystemMemorySize64","PeakPa
gedMemorySize

","PeakPagedMemorySize64","PeakWorkingSet","PeakWorki
ngSet64","PeakVirtualMemorySize","PeakVirtualMemorySi
ze64","Priori

tyBoostEnabled","PriorityClass","PrivateMemorySize","
PrivateMemorySize64","PrivilegedProcessorTime","Proce
ssName","Proc

essorAffinity","Responding","SessionId","StartInfo","
StartTime","SynchronizingObject","Threads","TotalProc
essorTime","U

serProcessorTime","VirtualMemorySize","VirtualMemoryS
ize64","EnableRaisingEvents","StandardInput","Standar
dOutput","Sta
```

```
ndardError","WorkingSet","WorkingSet64","Site","Conta
iner"

"Process","powershell","216","597544960","60399616","
63197184","21692","C:\WINDOWS\system32\WindowsPowerSh
ell\v1.0\powe

rshell.exe","Microsoft
Corporation","3.4788223","6.1.6587.1
(fbl_srv_powershell(nigels).070711-
0102)","6.1.6587.1","Win

dows PowerShell","Microsoft® Windows® Operating
System","8",,"False",,"860","216","5132",".","5636936
","Windows PowerSh

ell 2.0 (04/17/2008
00:10:40)","System.Diagnostics.ProcessModule
(powershell.exe)","1413120","204800","System.Diagnost
i

cs.ProcessModuleCollection","21692","21692","63197184
","63197184","320080","320080","63868928","63868928",
"60715008","6

0715008","598642688","598642688","True","Normal","631
97184","63197184","00:00:00.2028013","powershell","15
","True","1",

"System.Diagnostics.ProcessStartInfo","4/21/2008
3:49:19
PM",,"System.Diagnostics.ProcessThreadCollection","00
:00:03.51
```

```
00225","00:00:03.3072212","597544960","597544960","Fa
lse",,,,"60399616","60399616",,
```

This rather long command will convert one process object into a CSV format. It makes use of the Get-Process cmdlet to put the PowerShell process onto the local computer; then it will use the pipeline operator to send the command over to ConvertTo-CSV and this then coverts to a group of strings, separated by commas.

Example 2

```
PS C:\> $date = get-date

PS C:\> convertto-csv -inputobject $date -delimiter
";" -notypeinformation
```

This command will convert a date object into CSV

The first example used the Get-Date cmdlet as a way of getting the current date and then saves it in the variable called $date.

The second example used the ConvertTo-CSV cmdlet as a way of converting a DateTime object, located in the variable $date, into CSV. The command makes use of the InputObject parameter so that the object that needs to be converted can be specified. The Delimiter parameter is used to specify the delimiter to be used in separating each of the object properties and the NoTypeInformation parameter is used to suppress the #TYPE string.

The Import-CSV cmdlet will create objects that are table-like from the items it gets from the CSV. Each CSV file column will become a property of a custom object and the row items will become the property values. Import-CSV will work on any CSV file, including those that have been generated by the Export-CSV cmdlet.

The parameters of Import-CSV can be used to specify the item delimiter and the column header row, or to instruct Import-CSV to use the list separator item delimiter for the current culture.

The ConvertFrom and ConvertTo-CSV cmdlets can also be used to convert objects into CSV strings and vice versa. Both are the same as the Export-CSV and the Import-CSV cmdlets with the exception they don't deal with files.

From PowerShell 3 onwards, if there is a null or an empty value in a CSV file header row entry, PowerShell will insert a default header row name and will display a warning message. Before PowerShell 3, an empty or null value would result in the Import-CSV command failing. Let's look at a couple of examples:

Example 1

This first example will show you how to export a CSV object file and then import it. The first command will use the Get-Process cmdlet to put the process onto a local computer and then the pipeline operator to send the process objects over to the Export-CSV cmdlet. That cmdlet will then export the objects to a file in the current directory called Processes.CSV.

```
PS C:\> get-process | export-csv processes.csv
```

The second example shows the Import-CSV cmdlet being used to import processes that are in the Import-CSV file. The resulting objects are them saved in the variable called $p.

```
PS C:\> $p = Import-Csv processes.csv
```

The third example shows a pipeline operator being used to pipe the objects that have ben imported into the Get-Member cmdlet. The result will show the process objects are CSV:System.Diagnostic.Process and not the System.Diagnostic.Process objects that Get-Process will return. Also, note that, as there is no entry type present in the format files for the CSV process objects, these objects are not going to be formatted in the same way that the standard process objects would be formatted. If you want to display the objects, you must use the right formatting cmdlets, like Format-List, Format-Table, etc., or you must pipe the objects to the Out-GridView cmdlet.

Example 1

The next example shows you how to export a CSV object file and then import it:

```
PS C:\> $p | get-member

TypeName: CSV:System.Diagnostics.Process

Name                          MemberType   Definition

----                          ----------   ----------

Equals                        Method
System.Boolean Equals(Object obj)

GetHashCode                   Method       System.Int32
GetHashCode()

GetType                       Method       System.Type
GetType()

ToString                      Method       System.String
ToString()

BasePriority                  NoteProperty System.String
BasePriority=8

Company                       NoteProperty System.String
Company=Microsoft Corporation

...

PS C:\> $p | out-gridview
```

Example 2

This last example shows you how to use the Delimiter parameter from the Import-CSV cmdlet, and shows you how to export processes to a file that uses the colon delimiter:

```
PS C:\> get-process | export-csv processes.csv -
Delimiter :

PS C:\> $p = Import-Csv processes.csv -Delimiter :
```

When you import, the Import-CSV file will use the delimiter parameter to show which delimiter is being used in the file.

Chapter 6
Making PowerShell Work for You

As I have already said, you cannot learn PowerShell in just a few minutes. There is a lot to learn and it will take a great deal of concentration, hard work and a lot of practice to learn it. It is worth it to put in the work because, once you have PowerShell working how you want it to, you will seriously wonder how you did without it before. This is an overview of how PowerShell can work for you:

Working with Processes

There are Process cmdlets in PowerShell that you can use to manage both remote and local processes within PowerShell.

- **Getting Processes (Get-Process)**

If you want to get the processes that are running on the local computer, you would run Get-Process without specifying any parameters. If you want specific processes, you will need to specify the process ID or the process name. The following example shows you how to get the Idle process:

```
PS> Get-Process -id 0

Handles  NPM(K)    PM(K)      WS(K) VM(M)   CPU(s)
Id ProcessName

-------  ------    -----      ----- -----   ------
-- -----------

      0       0        0         16     0
0 Idle
```

Although it is normal practice for a cmdlet not to return any data in certain situations, if you use Get-Process with a ProcessID to specify a process, an error will be returned if there are no matches. This is because, usually, a known-running process is retrieved but, if there is no process with the specified ID, it is more than likely that the ID is either incorrect or that the process has exited already:

```
PS> Get-Process -Id 99

Get-Process : No process with process ID 99 was
found.

At line:1 char:12

+ Get-Process  <<<< -Id 99
```

If you want to specify a subset of processes that are based on a process name, you would use the Name parameter of the Get-Process cmdlet. This parameter is able to take several names in a list separated by commas and it also provides support for wildcards so you can use name patterns.

For example, this command will get those processes whose names start with "ex":

```
PS> Get-Process -Name ex*

Handles  NPM(K)    PM(K)      WS(K) VM(M)   CPU(s)
Id ProcessName

-------  ------    -----      ----- -----   ------
-- -----------

    234       7     5572      12484   134     2.98
1684 EXCEL

    555      15    34500      12384   134   105.25
728 explorer
```

The foundation for the PowerShell processes is .NET System.Diagnostics.Process class and it must follow several of the conventions that are used by System.Diagnstics.Process. One convention is that the name of a process for an executable will never have the .exe at the end of the name.

Get-Process is also able to accept several values for the Name parameter:

```
PS> Get-Process -Name exp*,power*

Handles  NPM(K)    PM(K)      WS(K) VM(M)   CPU(s)
Id ProcessName

-------  ------    -----      ----- -----   ------
-- -----------
```

```
    540        15     35172        48148    141      88.44
408 explorer

    605         9     30668        29800    155       7.11
3052 powershell
```

You may also use a parameter of Get-Process, called ComputerName, to get processes that are on remote computers. For example, you can use the following command to get PowerShell processes from the local computer (localhost) and from two remote computers.

```
PS> Get-Process -Name PowerShell -ComputerName
localhost, Server01, Server02

Handles  NPM(K)    PM(K)      WS(K) VM(M)   CPU(s)
Id ProcessName

-------  ------    -----      ----- -----   ------
-- -----------

    258         8    29772        38636    130
3700 powershell

    398        24    75988        76800    572
5816 powershell

    605         9    30668        29800    155       7.11
3052 powershell
```

You can't see the computer names on the display but they are contained within the MachineName property of the processes that are returned by Get-Process. The next command shows how to use the cmdlet called Format-Table to display the ProcessName, process ID, and the MachineName properties of all the process objects:

```
PS> Get-Process -Name PowerShell -ComputerName
localhost, Server01, Server01 | Format-Table -
Property ID, ProcessName, MachineName

  Id ProcessName MachineName

  -- ----------- -----------

3700 powershell  Server01

3052 powershell  Server02

5816 powershell  localhost
```

The next command is more complex and it adds the MachineName property into the Get-Process display. The Backtick is the continuation character in PowerShell.

```
get-process powershell -computername localhost,
Server01, Server02 | format-table -property Handles,
`


@{Label="NPM(K)";Expression={[int]($_.NPM/1024)}}, `


@{Label="PM(K)";Expression={[int]($_.PM/1024)}}, `


@{Label="WS(K)";Expression={[int]($_.WS/1024)}}, `
```

```
@{Label="VM(M)";Expression={[int]($_.VM/1MB)}}, `
                    @{Label="CPU(s)";Expression={if
($_.CPU -ne $()`
                    {$_.CPU.ToString("N")}}}, `
                    Id, ProcessName, MachineName -
auto


Handles  NPM(K)  PM(K) WS(K) VM(M) CPU(s)   Id
ProcessName  MachineName

-------  ------  ----- ----- ----- ------   -- -------
----  -----------

    258       8  29772 38636   130          3700
powershell Server01

    398      24  75988 76800   572          5816
powershell localhost

    605       9  30668 29800   155 7.11     3052
powershell Server02
```

- **Stopping Processes (Stop-Process)**

PowerShell provides great flexibility in listing processes but what about if you want to stop a process? For that, we use the Stop-Process cmdlet to take an ID or a name to specify which process you want stopping. Whether you can actually stop a process or not will depend on your permissions and there are processes that simply can't be stopped. For example, if you were to try stopping the Idle process, you would see an error:

```
PS> Stop-Process -Name Idle

Stop-Process : Process 'Idle (0)' cannot be stopped due to the following error:

 Access is denied

At line:1 char:13

+ Stop-Process  <<<< -Name Idle
```

You can also use the Confirm parameter to force prompting. This parameter is very useful when you use wildcards for when you are specifying process names, simply because you may match processes accidentally that you do not want to be stopped:

```
PS> Stop-Process -Name t*,e* -Confirm

Confirm

Are you sure you want to perform this action?

Performing operation "Stop-Process" on Target "explorer (408)".

[Y] Yes  [A] Yes to All  [N] No  [L] No to All  [S] Suspend  [?] Help

(default is "Y"):n
```

```
Confirm

Are you sure you want to perform this action?

Performing operation "Stop-Process" on Target
"taskmgr (4072)".

[Y] Yes  [A] Yes to All  [N] No  [L] No to All  [S]
Suspend  [?] Help

(default is "Y"):n
```

It is possible to perform complex manipulations of processes by using object filtering cmdlets. Because process objects contain Resounding properties that are true when they no longer respond, you can use the following command to stop any unresponsive application:

```
Get-Process | Where-Object -FilterScript
{$_.Responding -eq $false} | Stop-Process
```

The same approach could be used in other situations. For example, a secondary notification area application runs automatically when another application is started by the user. This may not work correctly in Terminal Services sessions but you still need it in the sessions that are being run on the physical computer console sessions. Sessions that are connected to the physical desktop will always have a session ID of 0, so that means that you can stop all instances of a process that are being used in other sessions and you do this through the use of the Where-Object and the SessionID process:

```
Get-Process -Name BadApp | Where-Object -FilterScript
{$_.SessionId -neq 0} | Stop-Process
```

There is no ComputerName parameter for the Stop-Process cmdlet. Because of this, you must use Invoke-Command to stop a process command on a remote computer. For example, if you wanted to stop the PowerShell process on the remote computer called Server01, you would use this command:

```
Invoke-Command -ComputerName Server01 {Stop-Process
Powershell}
```

PowerShell and WMI

Windows Management Instrumentation (WMI) is the core technology for system administration because it can show a large amount of information in a uniform way. Because WMI makes so much possible, one of the most useful cmdlets in PowerShell for accessing WMI objects is Get-WmiObject. In this part, we are going to look at how to use Get-WmiObject to access any WMI object and then use those objects to do specific things.

Listing WMI Classes

The first problem that anyone using WMI is likely to encounter is working out what they can do with WMI. The WMI classes, of which there are, quite literally, hundreds, some containing dozens of different properties, are used to describe the resources you can manage. The cmdlet, Get-WmiObject, helps you by making WMI discoverable and, if you type the following command you can see a whole list of all the WMI classes on the local computer:

```
PS> Get-WmiObject -List


__SecurityRelatedClass                              __NTLMUser9X

__PARAMETERS
__SystemSecurity

__NotifyStatus
__ExtendedStatus

Win32_PrivilegesStatus
Win32_TSNetworkAdapterSettingError

Win32_TSRemoteControlSettingError
Win32_TSEnvironmentSettingError

...
```

You can also get this same information off a remote computer by using the parameter called ComputerName and by specifying an IP address or a computer name:

```
PS> Get-WmiObject -List -ComputerName 192.168.1.29


__SystemClass                                        __NAMESPACE

__Provider
__Win32Provider

__ProviderRegistration
__ObjectProviderRegistration

...
```

The listing of classes returned by a remote computer will vary, according to the operating system that is being run on the computer and the specific WMI installations that have been added by applications that are installed.

Note – When you use Get-WmiObject to connect to remote computers, the remote computer has to be running WMI. Also, in the default configuration, the account you use must be included in the local admin group that is on the remote computer. However, you don't need to have PowerShell installed on the remote computer and this lets you administer systems that have WMI but not PowerShell.

You may even add the ComputerName when you are connecting to a local system. You can use the IP address, a loopback address of 127.0.0.1, the local computer name or the WMI-style '.' as the name of the computer. For example, if you have PowerShell on a computer called Admin01, showing an IP address of 192.168.1.90, you would use the following commands to return all of the WMI classes for that computer:

- `Get-WmiObject -List`
- `Get-WmiObject -List -ComputerName .`
- `Get-WmiObject -List -ComputerName Admin01`
- `Get-WmiObject -List -ComputerName 192.168.1.90`
- `Get-WmiObject -List -ComputerName 127.0.0.1`
- `Get-WmiObject -List -ComputerName localhost`

Get-WmiObject makes use of the namespace called root/cimv2 but, if you wanted to specify a different WMI namespace, you would use the NameSpace parameter and you would specify the namespace path that corresponds to it:

```
PS> Get-WmiObject -List -ComputerName 192.168.1.29 -
Namespace root


__SystemClass                                  __NAMESPACE

__Provider
__Win32Provider

...
```

Displaying WMI Class Details

If you already know what the name of the WMI class is, you may use it to gain the information you need straight away.

For example, the Win32_OperatingSystem is one of the WMI classes that is commonly used to get information about a computer:

```
PS> Get-WmiObject -Class Win32_OperatingSystem -
Namespace root/cimv2 -ComputerName .


SystemDirectory : C:\WINDOWS\system32

Organization    : Global Network Solutions

BuildNumber     : 2600

RegisteredUser  : Oliver W. Jones

SerialNumber    : 12345-678-9012345-67890

Version         : 5.1.2600
```

Although all parameters are shown, the command may be expressed in a better way. The parameter called ComputerName does not need to be used when you are connecting to the local system; it is just shown as a way of demonstrating a general case and remind you that the parameter is there if you need it. The Namespace will default to root/cimv2 and it too can be left out. Lastly, most of the PowerShell cmdlets let you leave out the name of most of the common parameters. For example, if you do not specify a name for the first parameter of Get-WMIObject, PowerShell will treat it as the Class Parameter. What that means is that you could issue the last command by typing:

```
Get-WmiObject Win32_OperatingSystem
```

There are many properties of the Win32_Operating system than what we show here ad, if you want to see all of the properties, you can use Get-Member; all properties are available as they are for any object property:

```
PS> Get-WmiObject -Class Win32_OperatingSystem -
Namespace root/cimv2 -ComputerName . | Get-Member -
MemberType Property


   TypeName:
System.Management.ManagementObject#root\cimv2\Win32_O
peratingSystem


Name                                        MemberType
Definition
----                                        ----------
----------
__CLASS                                     Property
System.String __CLASS {...
...
```

```
BootDevice                                          Property
System.String BootDevic...

BuildNumber                                         Property
System.String BuildNumb...

...
```

Displaying Non-Default Properties Using Format Cmdlets

If you wanted to get information that was contained within the Win32_OperatingSystem class that is now shown by default, you can use the Format cmdlets to show it. If, for example, you wanted to see the available memory data, you would type:

```
PS> Get-WmiObject -Class Win32_OperatingSystem -
Namespace root/cimv2 -ComputerName . | Format-Table -
Property
TotalVirtualMemorySize,TotalVisibleMemorySize,FreePhy
sicalMemory,FreeVirtualMemory,FreeSpaceInPagingFiles


TotalVirtualMemorySize TotalVisibleMem
FreePhysicalMem FreeVirtualMemory
FreeSpaceInPagingFiles
```

```
--------------- --------------- --------------- -----
---------- -------------

2097024          785904          305808
2056724         1558232
```

Note – Wildcards will work with a property name in the Format-Table cmdlet and, as such, you can reduce the final pipeline element to `Format-Table -Property TotalV*,Free*`

The memory data would probably be easier to read if you were to format it as a list and you would do this by typing:

```
PS> Get-WmiObject -Class Win32_OperatingSystem -
Namespace root/cimv2 -ComputerName . | Format-List
TotalVirtualMemorySize,TotalVisibleMemorySize,FreePhy
sicalMemory,FreeVirtualMemory,FreeSpaceInPagingFiles


TotalVirtualMemorySize : 2097024

TotalVisibleMemorySize : 785904

FreePhysicalMemory     : 301876

FreeVirtualMemory      : 2056724

FreeSpaceInPagingFiles : 1556644
```

PowerShell v5

PowerShell 5 includes some significant features that improve how you use it, extend its use and let you control Windows-based environments more comprehensively. It is backward-compatible; all providers, cmdlets, snapins, modules, functions, scripts and profiles designed for PowerShell 4, 3 and 2 will usually work with PowerShell 5, without the need for any changes. You do not need to update to PowerShell 5 manually; if you are already running an earlier version, a Windows Update will provide the updated version for you. PowerShell updates are also automatic, leavening you free to do what you need to without the worry of whether you are up to date or not.

Major Features of v5

The notion of Desired State Configuration was introduced with Windows Server 2012 and PowerShell 5 takes it further through a new feature called OneGet. This feature is designed to simply the process of discovering and installing software to your computer. It is a brand-new module that allows you to install any of the hundreds of software packages that reside on the Chocolatey repository.

For those that don't know, Chocolatey is a Windows package manager, a framework for the installation of tools and applications that you need on your Windows computer. Chocolatey uses PowerShell as the means to deliver packages that are built on the Visual Studio, or NuGet infrastructure. OneGet allows you to:

- List the software repositories for each of the packages that you can install
- Manage those software repositories
- Search the repositories and filter them
- Use PowerShell to install and to uninstall packages from those repositories
- Learn how to use the Import-Module -Name OneGet command

You can also use one of a number of cmdlets for automating Ethernet ports and VLANS and, to reassure you, the only network switches that can be controlled with cmdlets for network switches ae those that have passed the Certified for Windows Program.

Windows Management Framework 5.0

WMF 5.0 contains updates pertaining to PowerShell ISE and PowerShell 5, including;

- Package Management cmdlets.
- Network Switch cmdlets.

Windows PowerShell Desired State Configuration (DSC)

The DSC in PowerShell is something akin to a function but, rather than scripting a process you instead specify Resource blocks and Nodes. To use DSC, you will need to have .NET Framework 4.5 installed and you should not test this on any production machine, especially one that is running Exchange Server.

Supported Operating Systems include:

- Windows 7
- Windows 8.1
- Windows Server 2008 R2
- Windows Server 2012
- Windows Server 2012 R2

Check Your Version of PowerShell with $Host

PowerShell 5 includes a simple command that lets you check which version of PowerShell you are running:

```
# Windows PowerShell Version Check
Clear-Host
$Host

Name:          Windows PowerShell ISE Host
Version:       5.0

InstanceId:        d36fdafd-f9e9-4642-bc85-
6dea29105f61
UI:            System.Management.Automation.
```

```
          Internal.Host.InternalHostUserInterface
CurrentCulture:   en-GB
CurrentUICulture: en-US
PrivateData:
   Microsoft.PowerShell.Host.ISE.ISEOptions
IsRunspacePushed:     False
Runspace:      System.Management.Automation.

          Runspaces.LocalRunspace
```

Chapter 7

PowerShell Terminology

When you begin to learn PowerShell, you will come across words and terms that you do not understand. While I have tried to explain them as I have used them throughout the book, it is perhaps better that the explanations are in one place, for easy reference. The following are the most common of the PowerShell terminology that you will come across;

Cmdlet

Pronounced "command-let", a cmdlet is the core execution unit of PowerShell. Think of it in terms of a small command that is used to do something. Cmdlets are compiled programs that are written in a .NET computer language, normally C# and they follow a simple VerboNoun naming convention, making them very easy to understand. The verb part of the name comes from a set of standard verbs and you can see these by running Get-Verb at the prompt in PowerShell. The noun part of the name is a singular version of the object that are trying to work with. Because of that, you can easily see what each cmdlet is going to do. If you want to see any of the cmdlets available, type in Get-Command.

Alias

An alias is a different name for a command in PowerShell. It could be a cmdlet, a Windows application or a PowerShell function. You can use the New-Alias cmdlet to make your own aliases. They are intended as a way of simplifying how much typing you need to do in the console; for example, instead of typing Get-Service, you would just type gsv instead. However, although it is a good way of streamlining your work in an interactive session, using aliases in PowerShell scripts is not recommended as they can often be somewhat cryptic; use of the full name is better and clearer.

Variable

Variables are containers, placeholders if you like. Variables are named similar to ComputerName but when you reference or access a variable in PowerShell it must be prefaced with the $ sign. Variables are used to better reference values that can change, such as numbers:

```
$i = 123
```

Now you can use the $i variable in any PowerShell expression

```
$i*2
```

The value of $1 can be changed and then the command run again. Variables are also used to hold the results of the command

```
$s = Get-Service | where {$_.status -eq 'running'}
```

The variable named S contains the output of the expression Get-Service, which is all the services running. The contents of $s can be accessed whenever you want and they can be used however you want, in the same way as if you ran the Get-Service expression.

Provider

Providers, sometimes called psprovider, are a part of PowerShell that makes it easy to use pretty much the same commands to access differing systems. Think of it as something like an interface a go-between for PowerShell and a bit of Windows, the File System and the Registry for example. A provider is a piece of software that can translate a cmdlet that is to be used with an underlying system. For example, PowerShell includes providers for the local registry and for the file system and you can use the same cmdlets, such as Get-ChildItem or Set-Location, to navigate through both. The provider works to translate the command the benefits to you include being able to use the same commands to navigate both the file system and the registry. By using the

Get-PSProvider cmdlet, you can see a list of all available providers.

Pipeline

The pipeline is the most important of all the concepts in PowerShell. The idea of it is not new, nor is it unique to PowerShell. It is a construct that helps objects pass from one command, normally a function or a cmdlet, to another and then on to another, until you have finished. The command has to be designed in such a way that it will accept a pipelined input but many of the PowerShell commands already have the right design. At the end of a pipeline, any remaining objects are displayed by PowerShell. One of the more interesting aspects of the pipeline is that you can start it with one object type and have a completely different one at the end. For example, you could have an expression that looks like this:

```
Get-Process | where {$_.ws -gt 100MB} | Measure-
Object -Property WS -Sum
```

At the start, a process object is being written to the pipeline but, by the end, a GenericMeasureInfo object is being written.

Script

PowerShell scripts are text files that have a ps1 extension; they are executed in the same way that a batch file is executed. Scripts are no more than a series of commands that are stored in a file and, when it is run, PowerShell wile execute every command in the file in the order it is written. Really there is little difference between running the commands in a script or interactively in the shell. Sometimes you can take commands from script files and copy and paste them into a session in the console; PowerShell will then run them.

Function

Functions are pieces of code that are designed with one purpose in mind. Think of a function as a cmdlet written in script version. You can create commands in a PowerShell script without the need to use Visual Studio for programming. Functions can be dead simple and they can be incredibly complex, like cmdlets, where they are able to accept a pipelined input, include help, have parameter validation and much more besides.

Module

Modules are PowerShell packages of commands that are related. Microsoft includes many of the commonly used commands as part of a number of modules. The cmdlet called Get-Module can be used to see what modules are available and what are already loaded but, before you can use any of the commands within a module, it has to be imported.

However, PowerShell now imports the module automatically when you first use a command contained within it. Provided you know which command you want to run, you don't really need to worry too much about modules.

Snapin

Snapins or pssnapin are command packaging types. This used to be how additional commands were delivered in the early days of PowerShell; they were packaged in a way that they needed to be installed and the registered on the computer before they could be used. To display all the loaded snapins and those that are registered, you use the Get-PSSnapin command. You won't really see too much of this these days as most extensions PowerShell come via modules but it is still useful to know what they are.

Conclusion

Thank you again for purchasing this book!

I hope this book was able to help you to have a better understanding of PowerShell, how to use it and what it can do for you.

The next step is to open *your* PowerShell and start playing! Play around with some of the code in this book, have a go at writing your own scripts and never worry about being wrong – you can always delete it and start again! There are plenty of other references on the internet for you to take your PowerShell skills further and the most important thing now is just to relax, enjoy yourself and learn all you can.

Finally, if you enjoyed this book, then I'd like to ask you for a favor, would you be kind enough to leave a review for this book on Amazon? It'd be greatly appreciated!

Thank you and good luck!

Made in the USA
Middletown, DE
18 April 2017